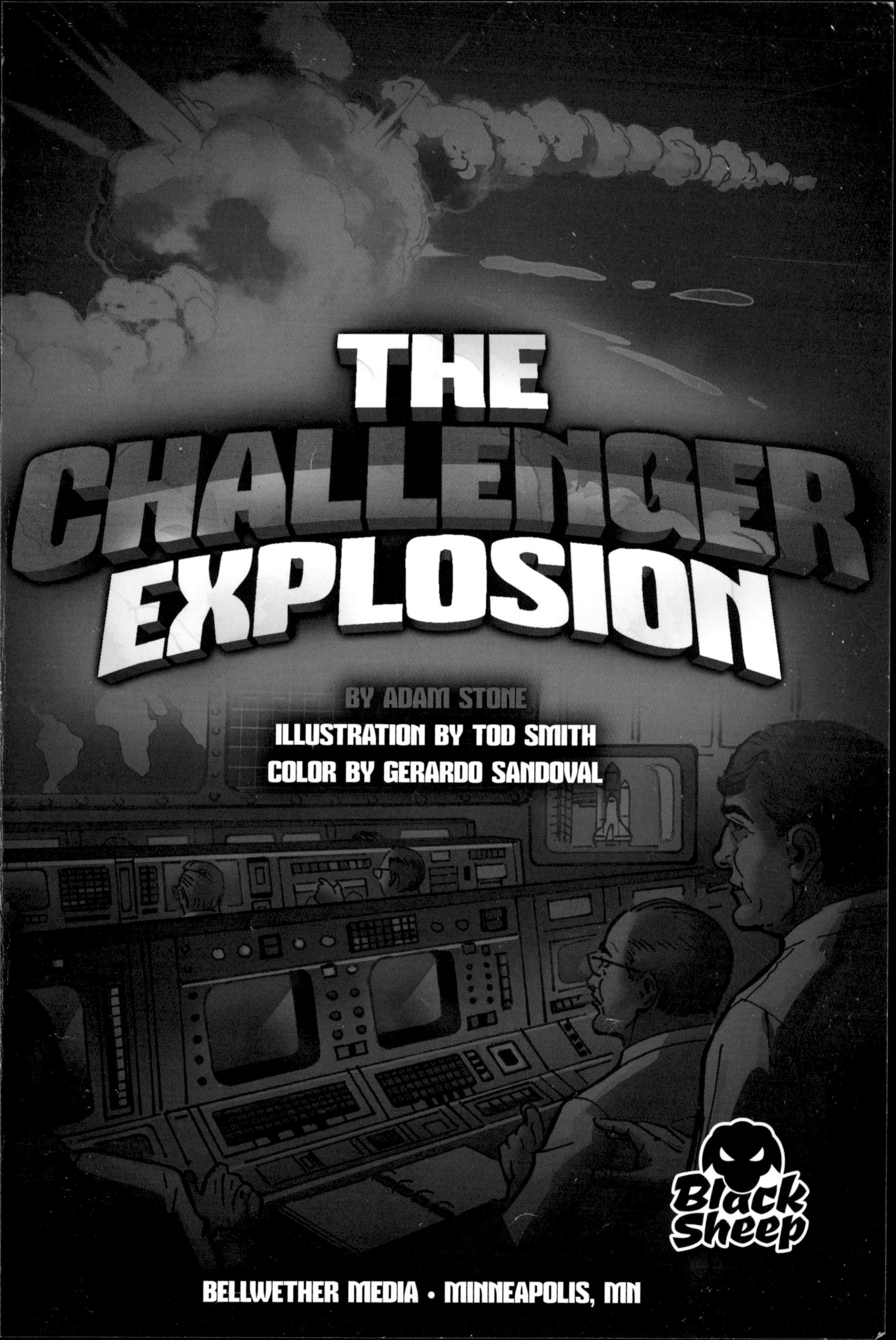

THE CHALLENGER EXPLOSION

BY ADAM STONE
ILLUSTRATION BY TOD SMITH
COLOR BY GERARDO SANDOVAL

Black Sheep

BELLWETHER MEDIA • MINNEAPOLIS, MN

STRAY FROM REGULAR READS
WITH BLACK SHEEP BOOKS.
FEEL A RUSH WITH EVERY READ!

Library of Congress Cataloging-in-Publication Data

Stone, Adam, author.
  The Challenger Explosion / by Adam Stone.
      pages cm. -- (Black Sheep. Disaster Stories)
  Includes bibliographical references and index.
  Summary: "Exciting illustrations follow the events of the Challenger explosion. The combination of brightly colored panels and leveled text is intended for students in grades 3 through 7"-- Provided by publisher.
  ISBN 978-1-62617-151-0 (hardcover : alk. paper)
  1. Challenger (Spacecraft)--Accidents--Juvenile literature. 2. Challenger (Spacecraft)--Accidents--Comic books, strips, etc. 3. Space vehicle accidents--United States--Juvenile literature. 4. Space vehicle accidents--United States--Comic books, strips, etc. 5. Space shuttles--Accidents--Juvenile literature. 6. Space shuttles--Accidents--Comic books, strips, etc. 7. Graphic novels. I. Title.
  TL867.S76 2014
  363.12'465--dc23
                              2014009033

This edition first published in 2015 by Bellwether Media, Inc.

No part of this publication may be reproduced in whole or in part without written permission of the publisher. For information regarding permission, write to Bellwether Media, Inc., Attention: Permissions Department, 5357 Penn Avenue South, Minneapolis, MN 55419.

Printed in the United States of America, North Mankato, MN.

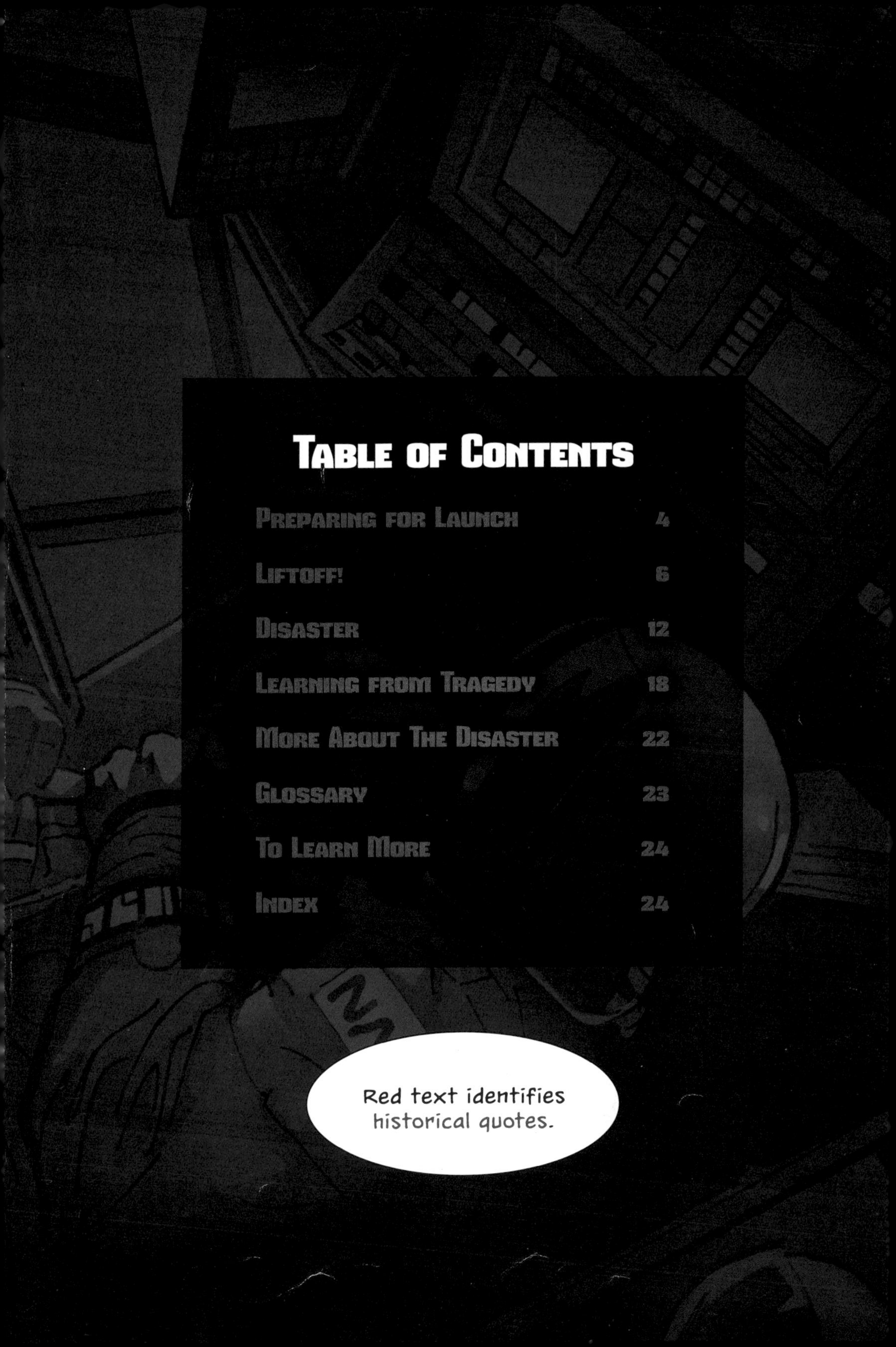

Table of Contents

Red text identifies historical quotes.

Preparing for Launch

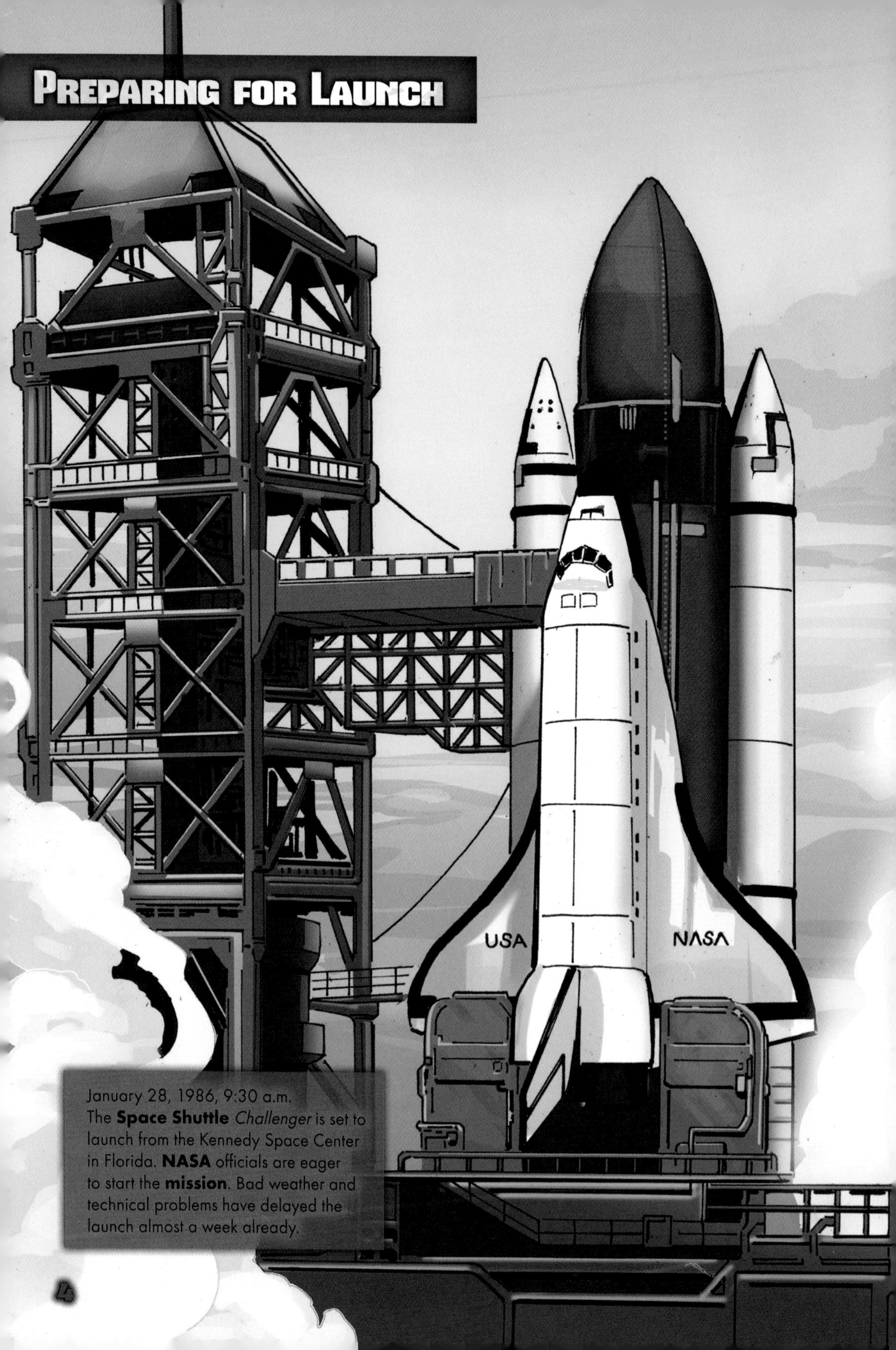
USA
NASA

January 28, 1986, 9:30 a.m.
The **Space Shuttle** *Challenger* is set to launch from the Kennedy Space Center in Florida. **NASA** officials are eager to start the **mission**. Bad weather and technical problems have delayed the launch almost a week already.

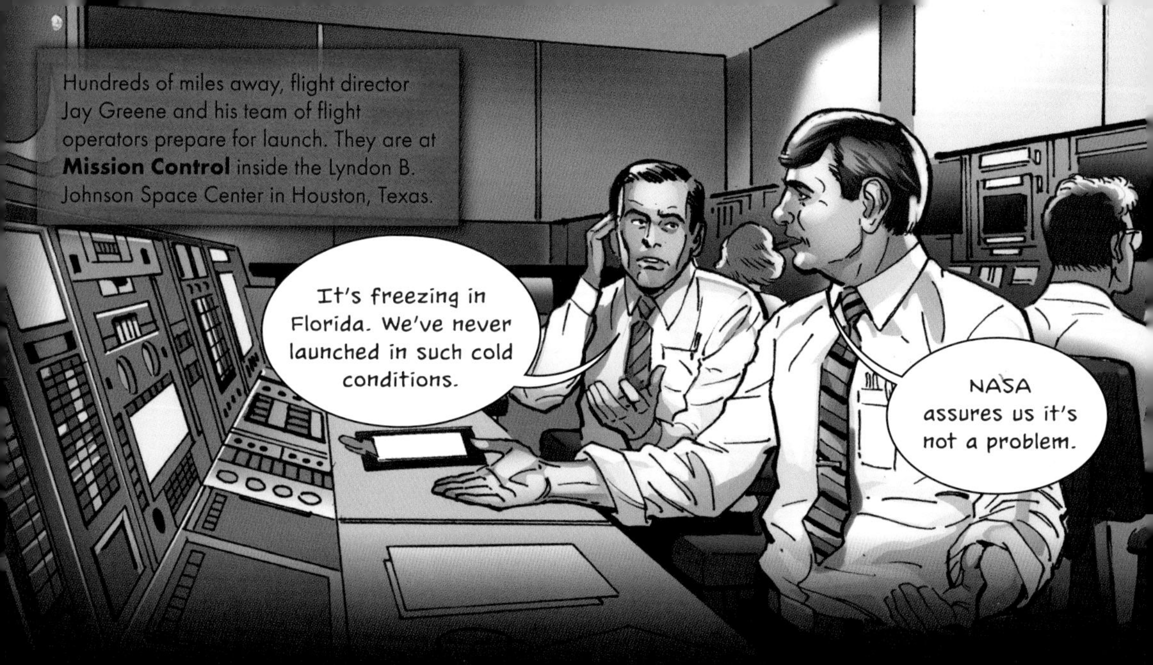
Hundreds of miles away, flight director Jay Greene and his team of flight operators prepare for launch. They are at **Mission Control** inside the Lyndon B. Johnson Space Center in Houston, Texas.
It's freezing in Florida. We've never launched in such cold conditions.
NASA assures us it's not a problem.

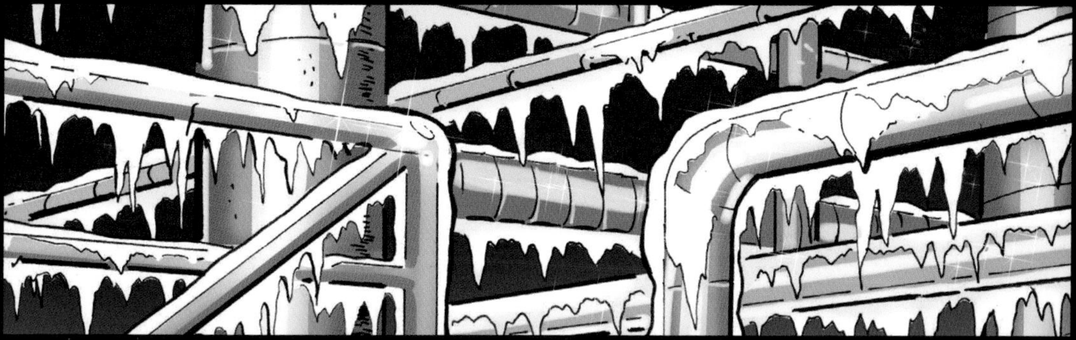

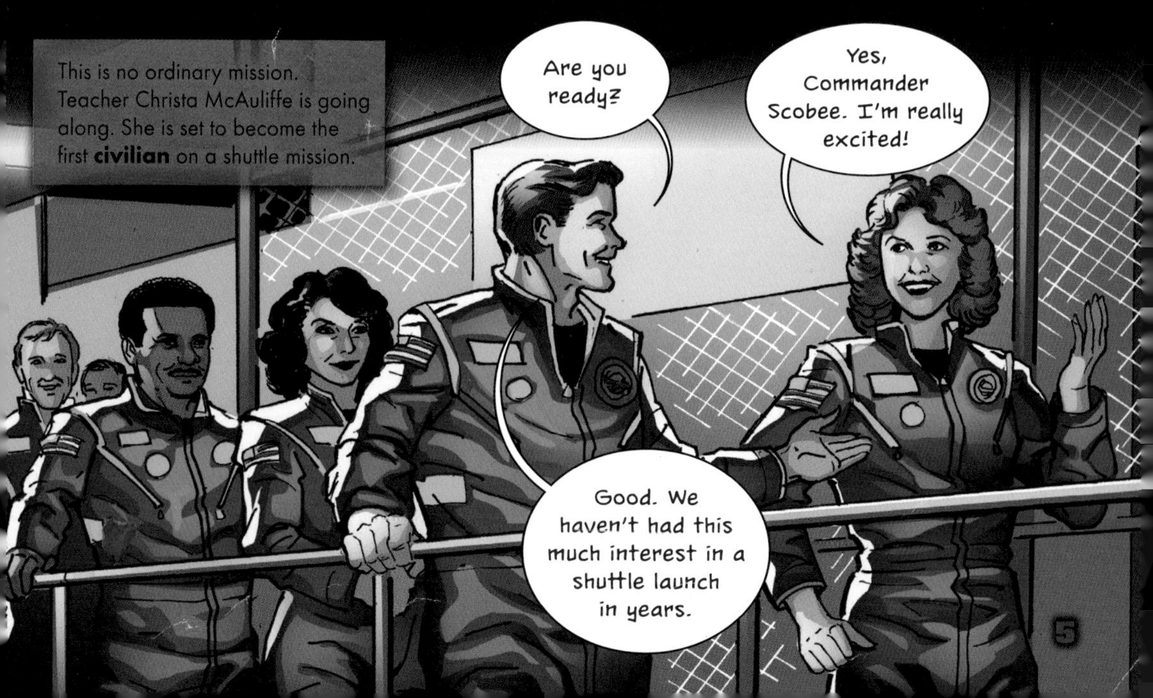
This is no ordinary mission. Teacher Christa McAuliffe is going along. She is set to become the first **civilian** on a shuttle mission.
Are you ready?
Yes, Commander Scobee. I'm really excited!
Good. We haven't had this much interest in a shuttle launch in years.

LIFTOFF!

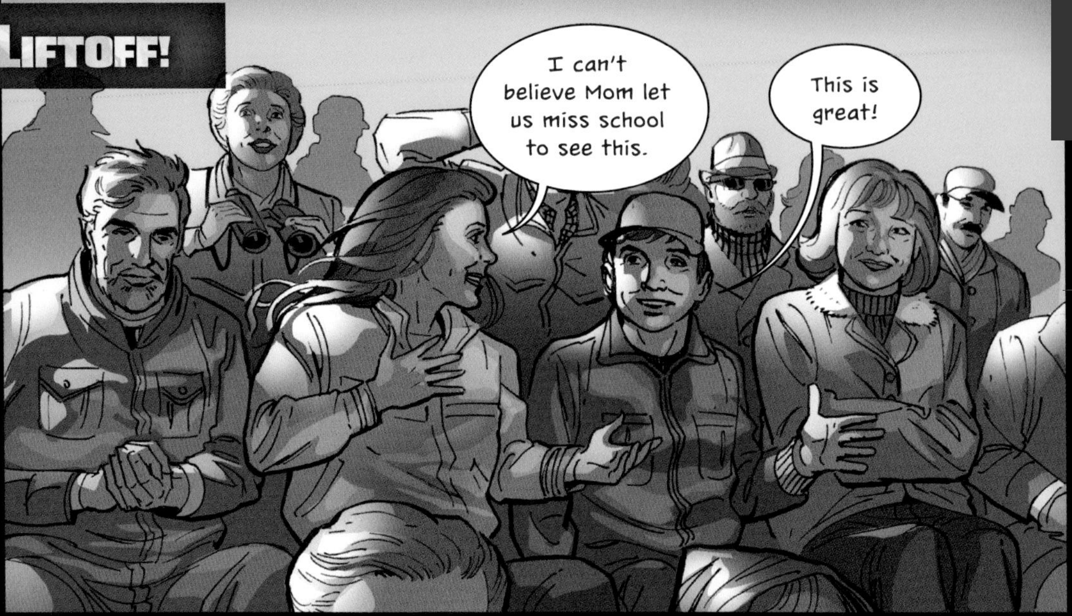
I can't believe Mom let us miss school to see this.
This is great!

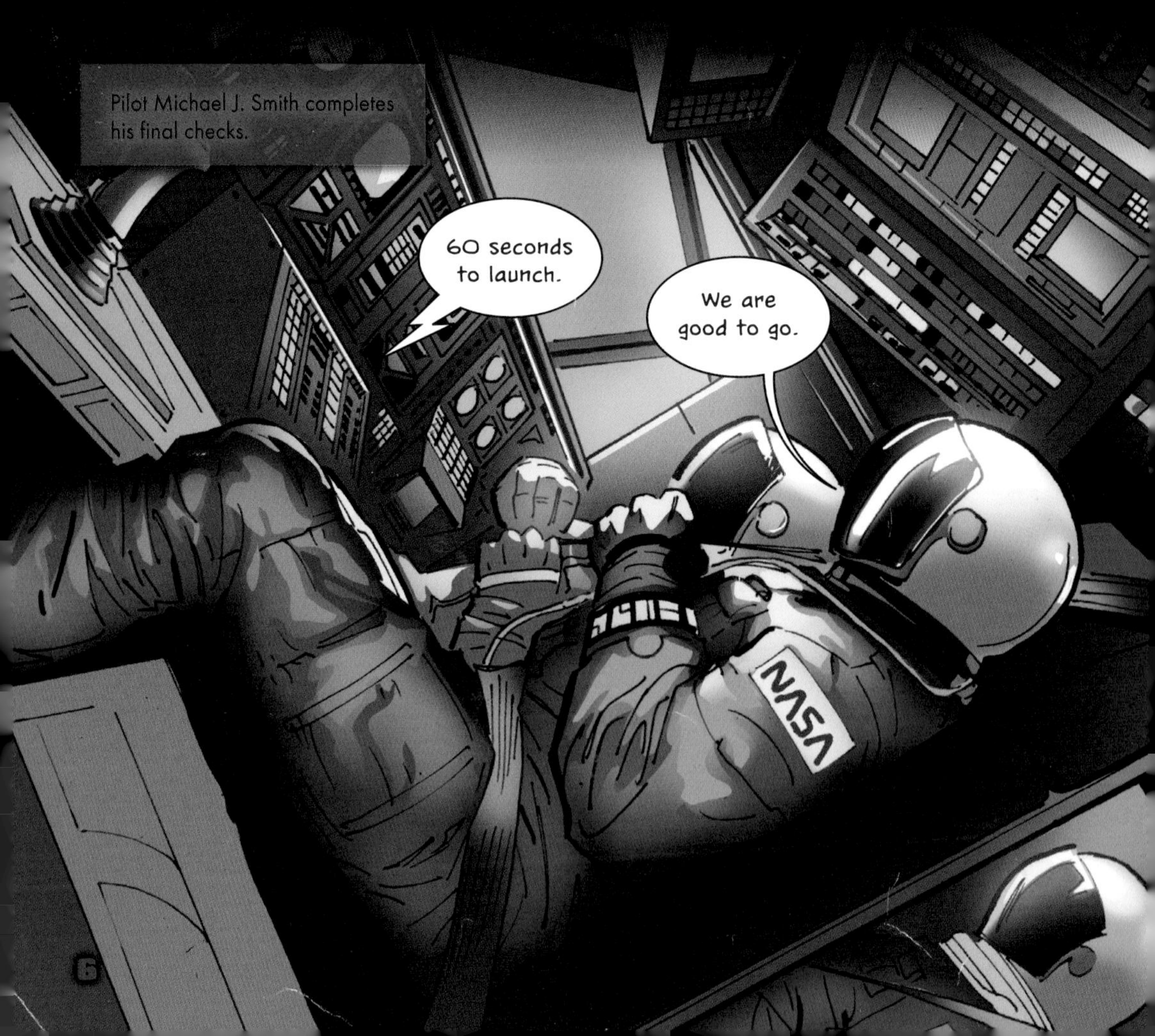
Pilot Michael J. Smith completes his final checks.
60 seconds to launch.
We are good to go.
NASA

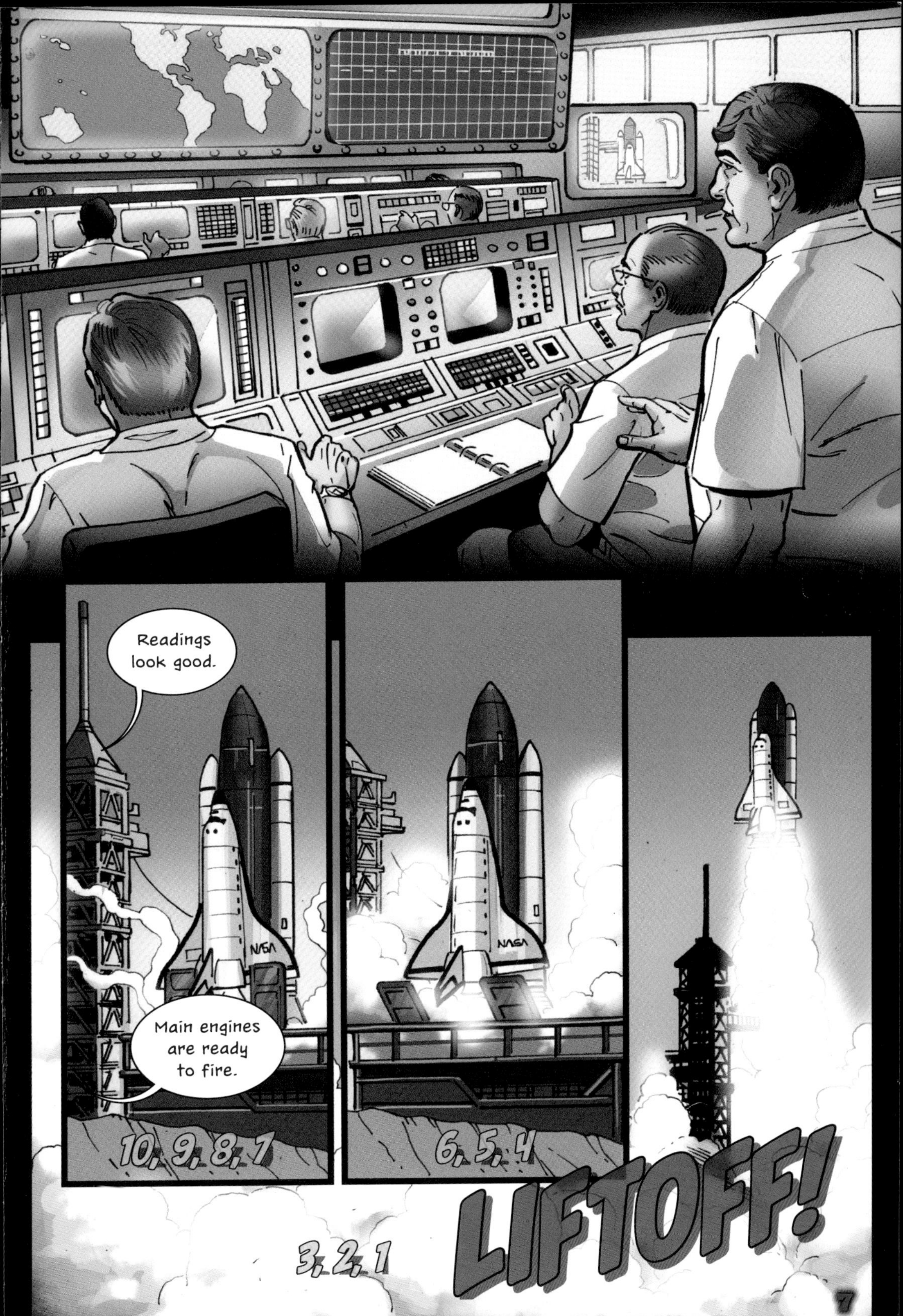

Readings look good.
Main engines are ready to fire.
10, 9, 8, 7
6, 5, 4
3, 2, 1
LIFTOFF!

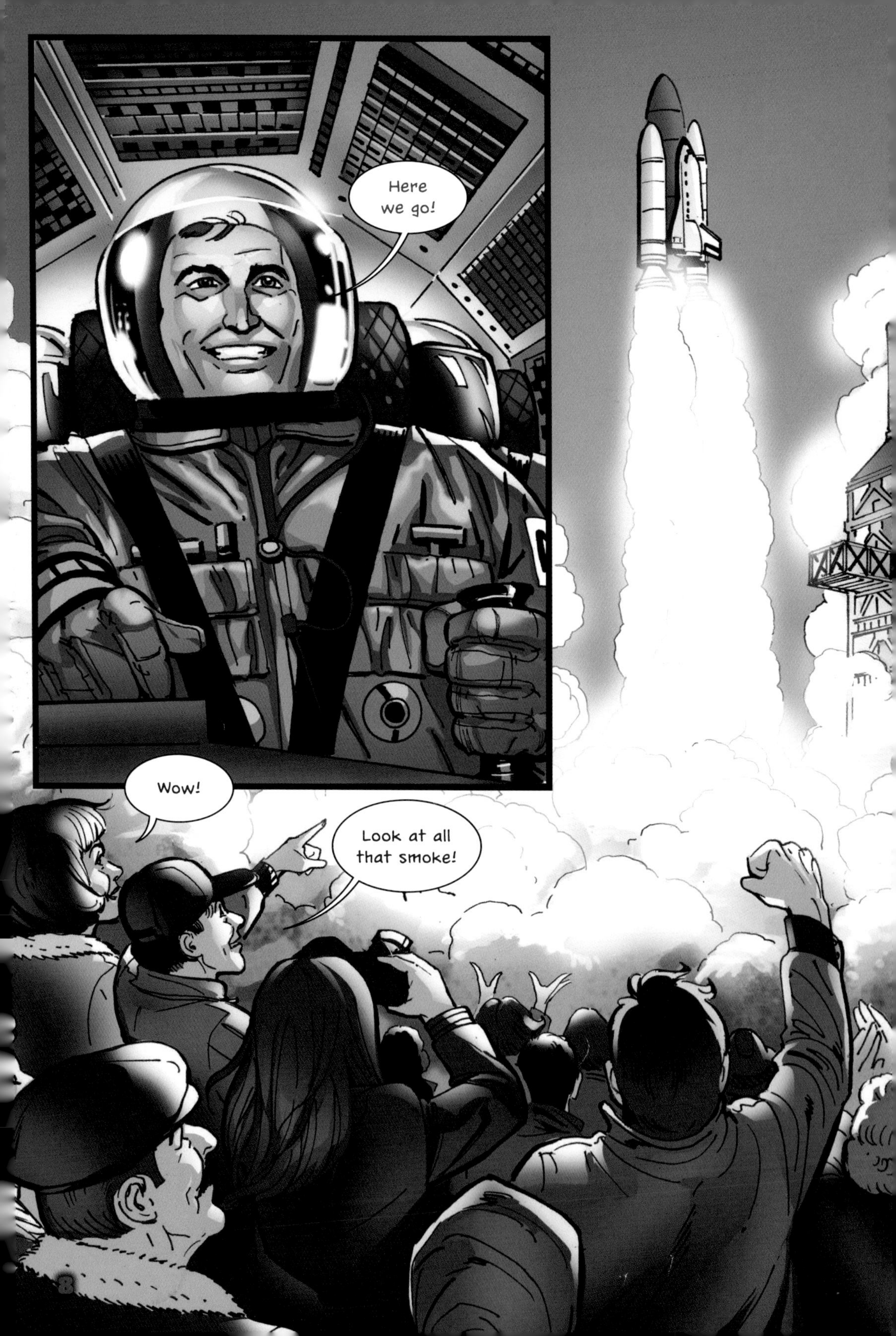
Here we go!
Wow!
Look at all that smoke!

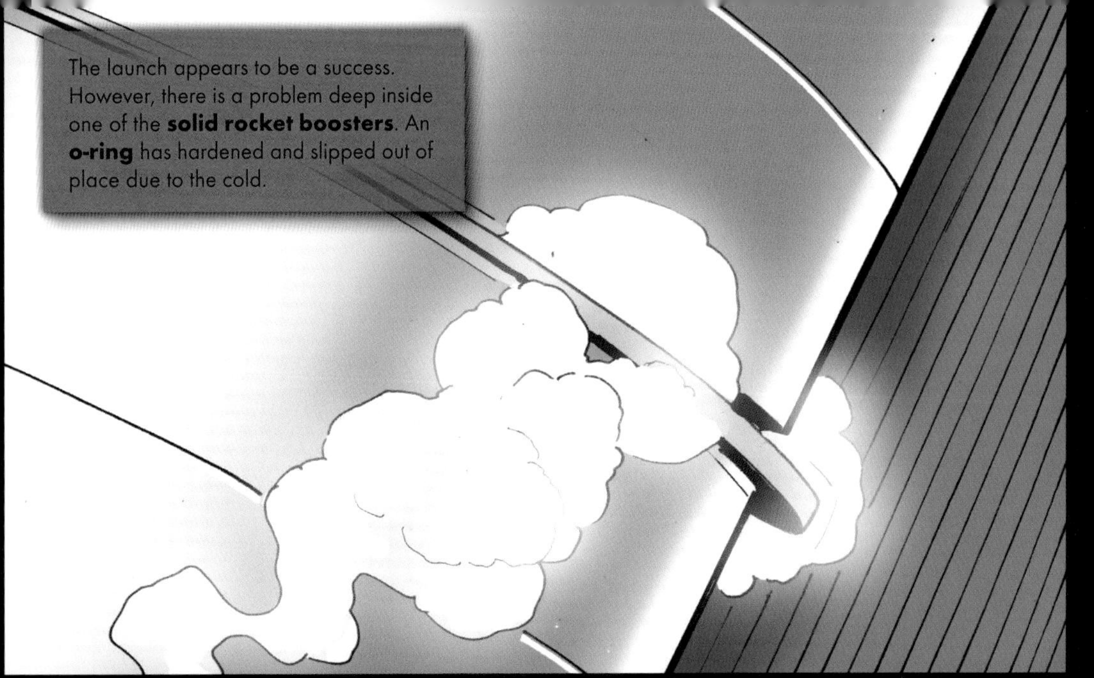
The launch appears to be a success. However, there is a problem deep inside one of the **solid rocket boosters**. An **o-ring** has hardened and slipped out of place due to the cold.

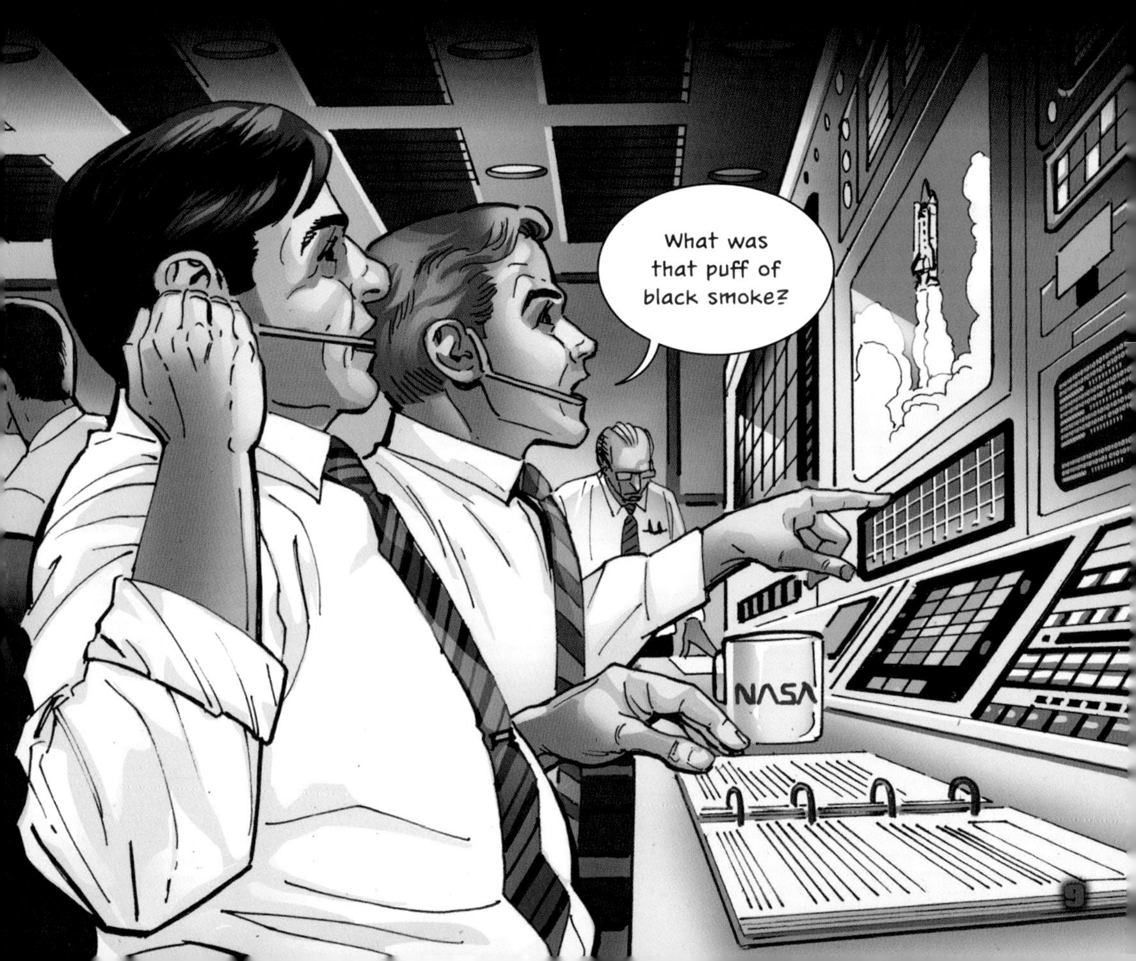
What was that puff of black smoke?
NASA

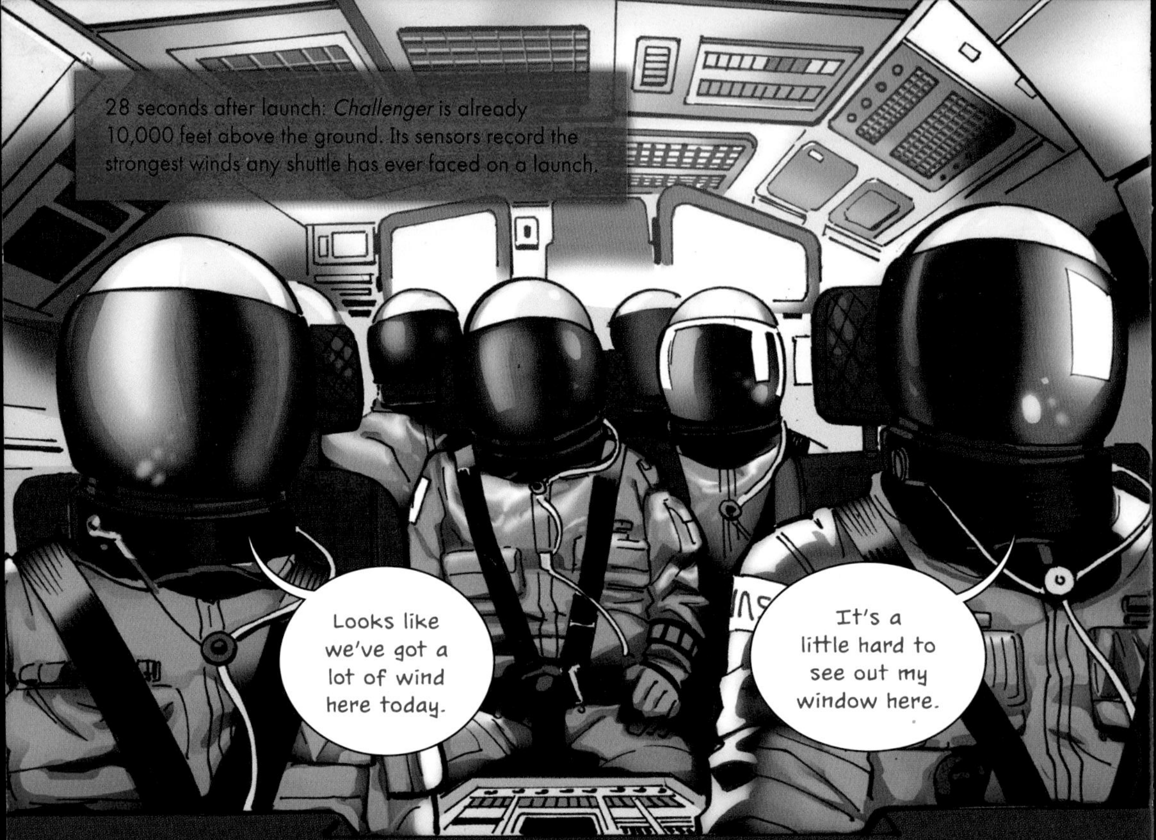
28 seconds after launch: *Challenger* is already 10,000 feet above the ground. Its sensors record the strongest winds any shuttle has ever faced on a launch.
Looks like we've got a lot of wind here today.
It's a little hard to see out my window here.

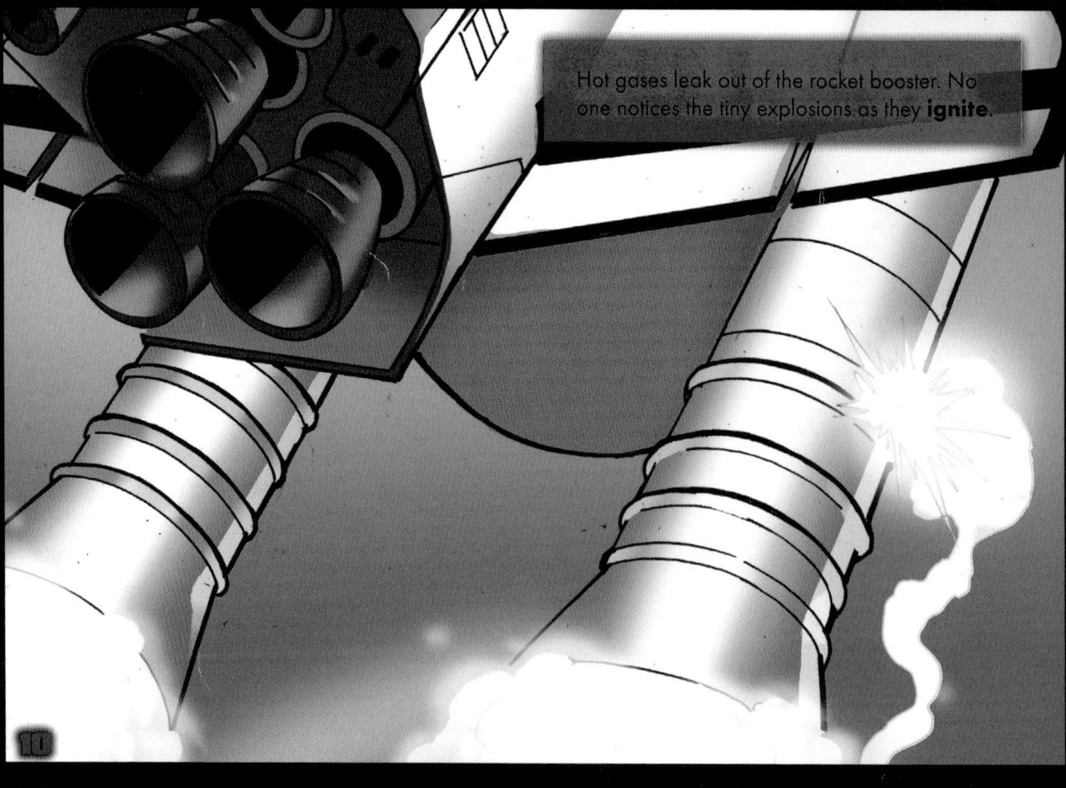
Hot gases leak out of the rocket booster. No one notices the tiny explosions as they **ignite**.

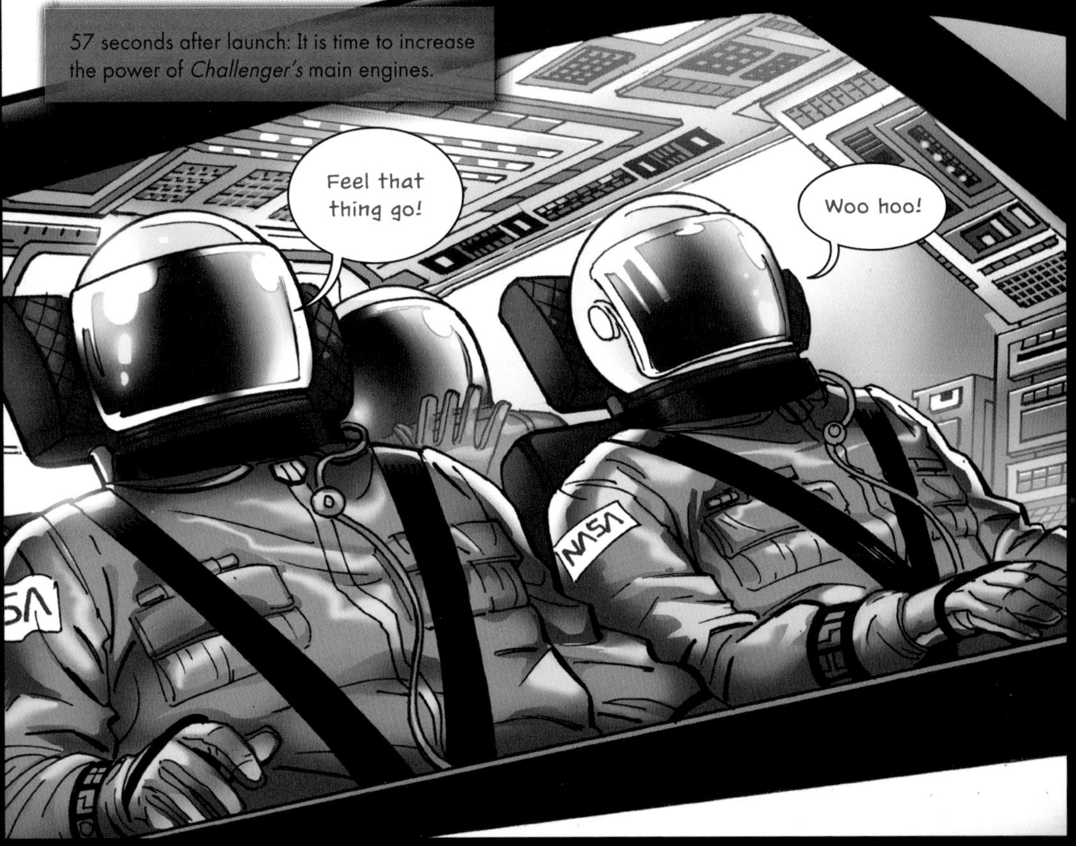
57 seconds after launch: It is time to increase the power of *Challenger's* main engines.
Feel that thing go!
Woo hoo!
NASA

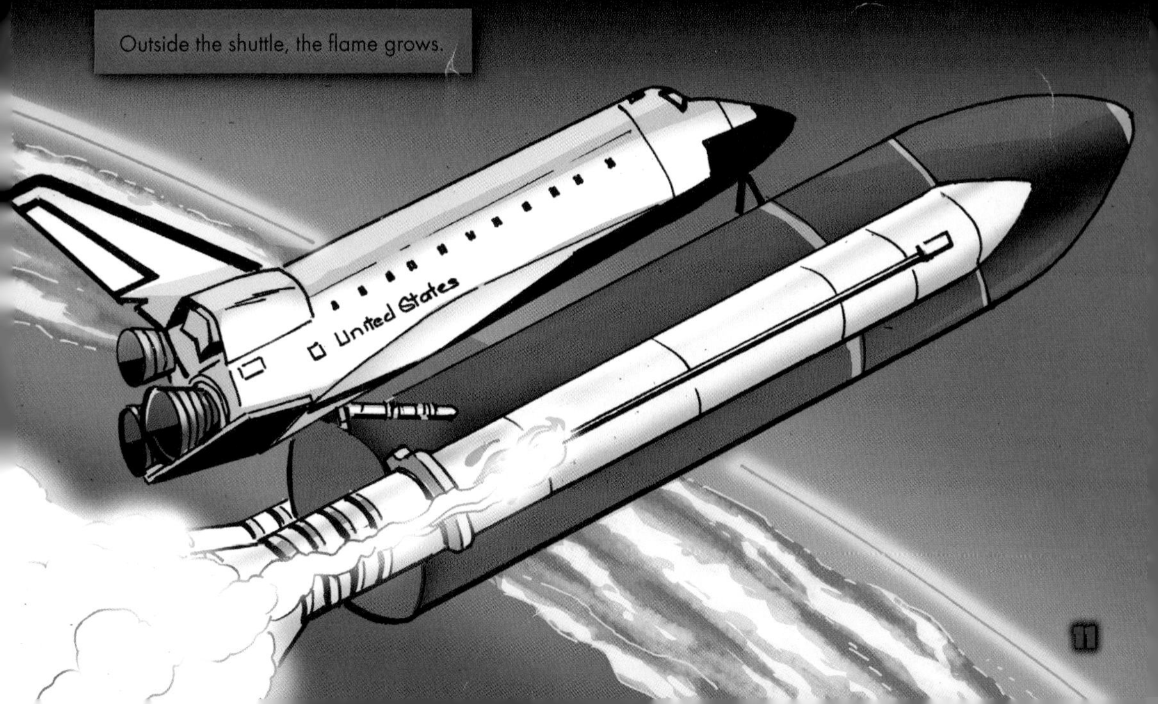
Outside the shuttle, the flame grows.
United States

Disaster

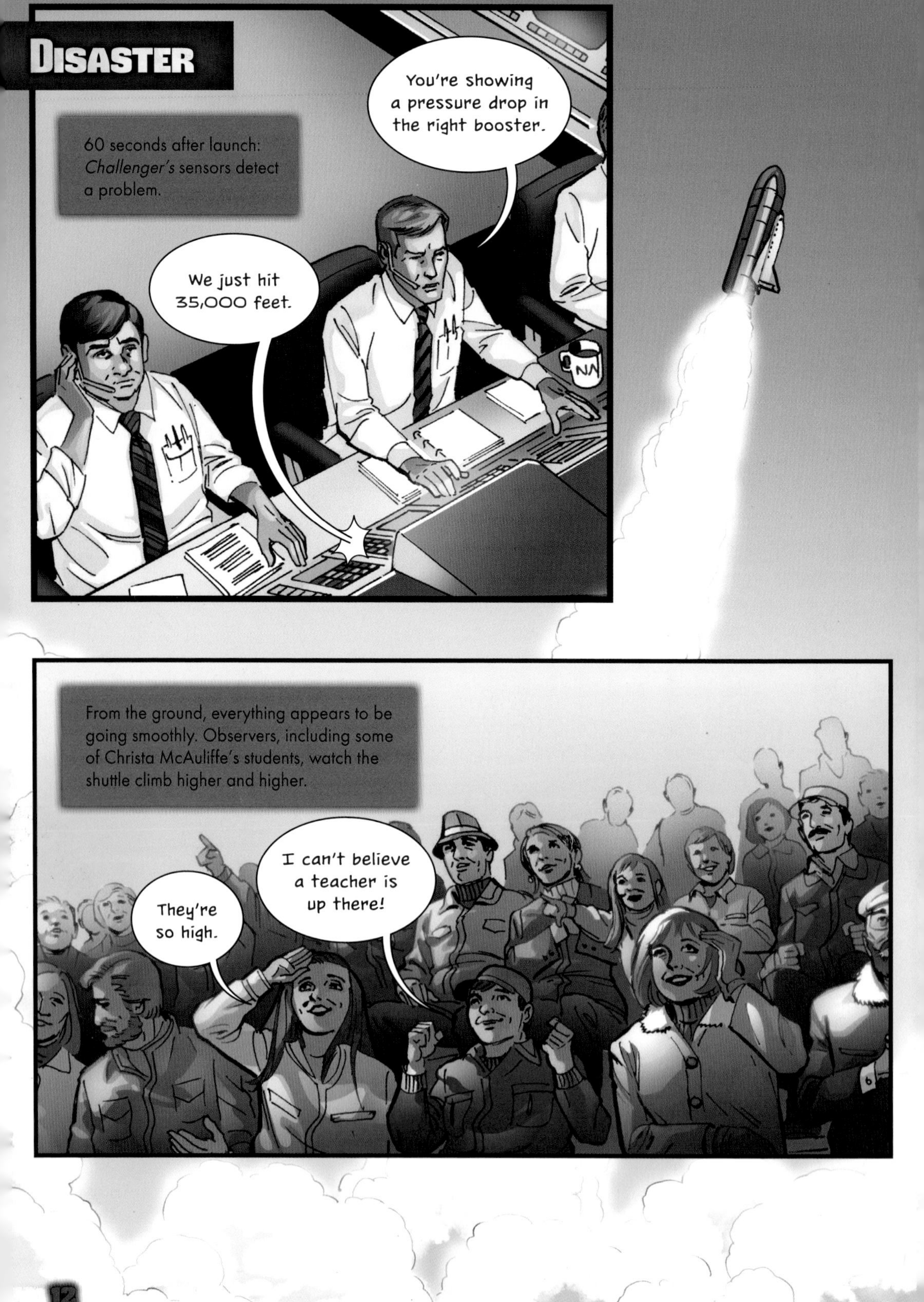
60 seconds after launch: *Challenger's* sensors detect a problem.
You're showing a pressure drop in the right booster.
We just hit 35,000 feet.
From the ground, everything appears to be going smoothly. Observers, including some of Christa McAuliffe's students, watch the shuttle climb higher and higher.
They're so high.
I can't believe a teacher is up there!

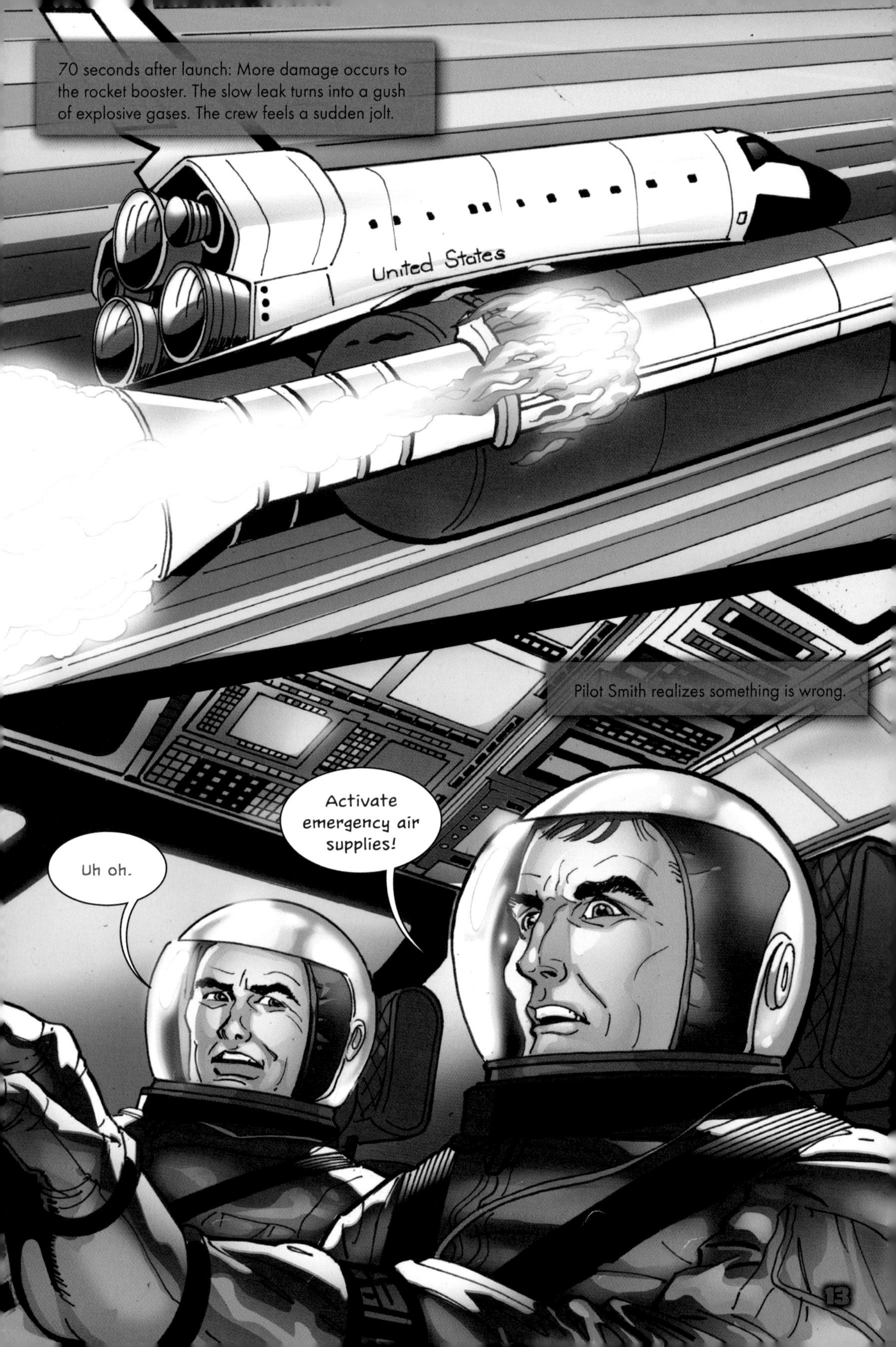
70 seconds after launch: More damage occurs to the rocket booster. The slow leak turns into a gush of explosive gases. The crew feels a sudden jolt.
United States
Pilot Smith realizes something is wrong.
Uh oh.
Activate emergency air supplies!

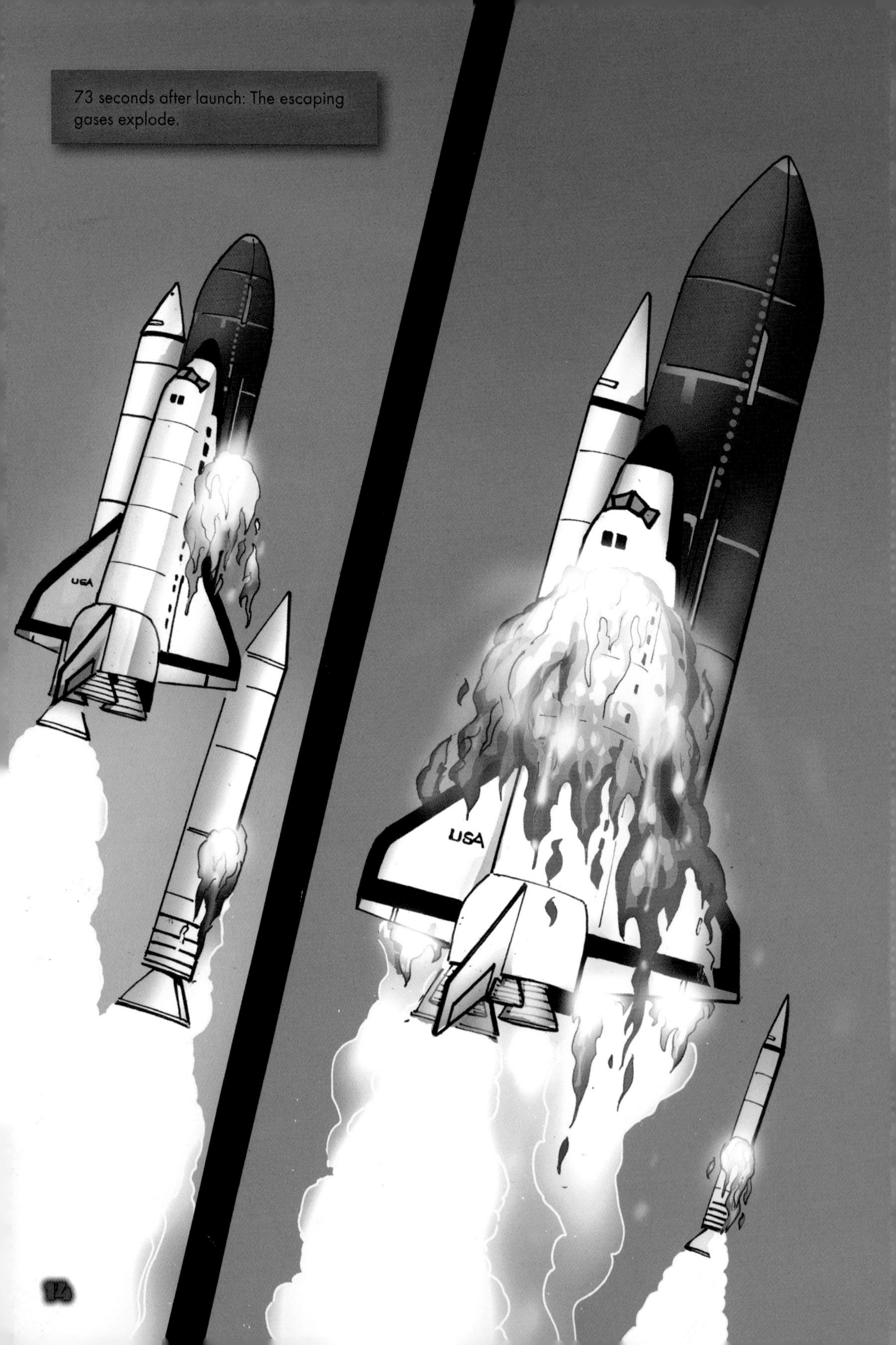
73 seconds after launch: The escaping gases explode.
USA
USA

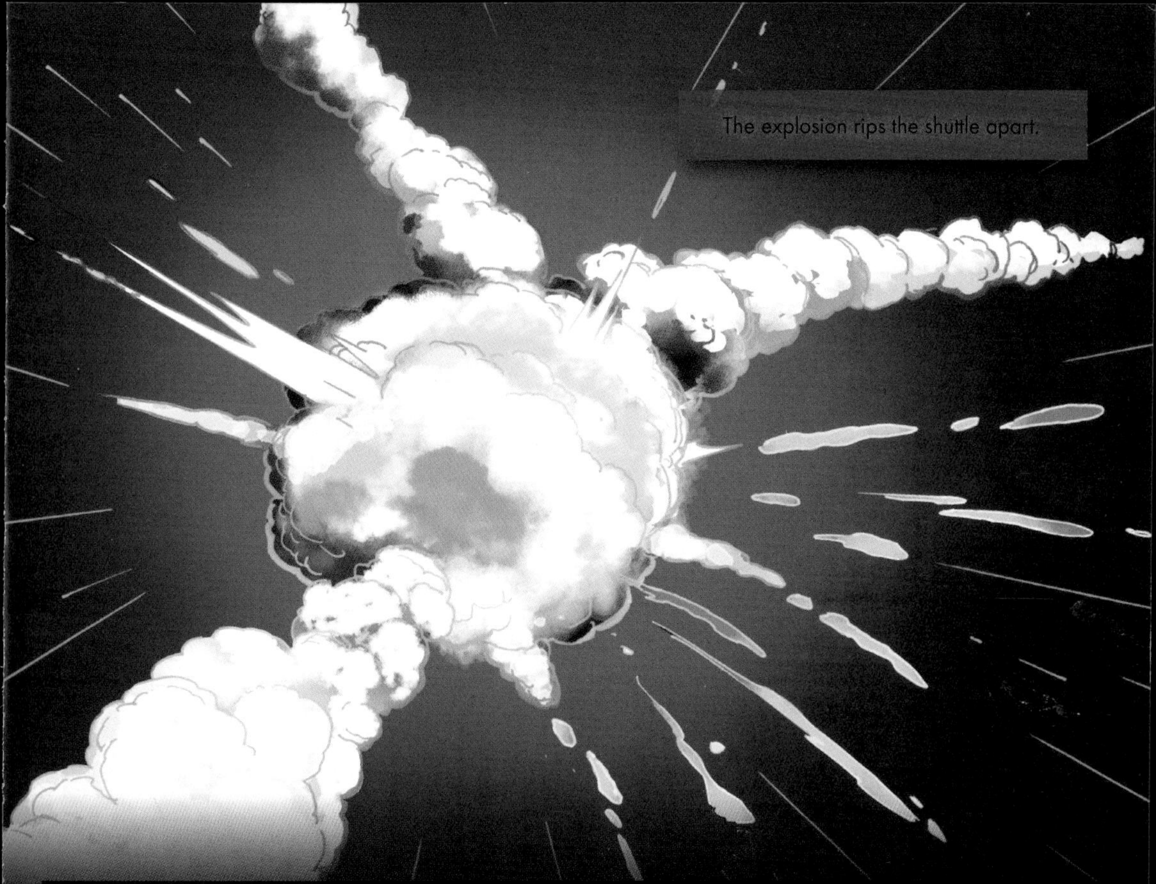
The explosion rips the shuttle apart.

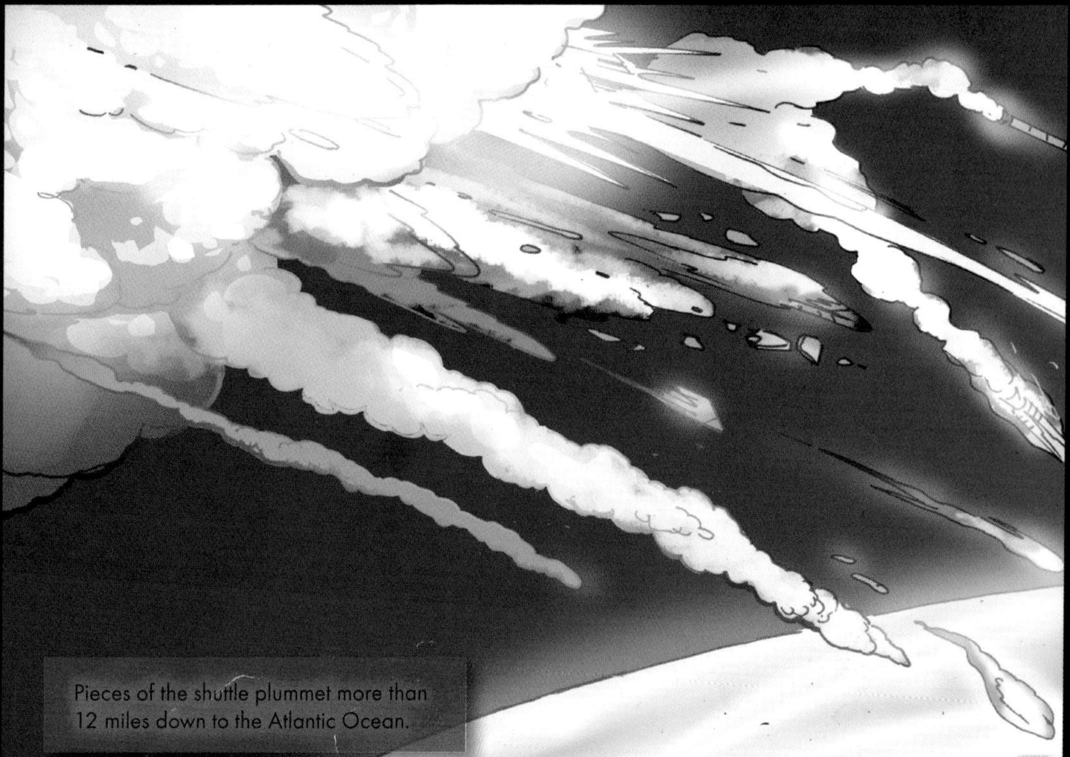
Pieces of the shuttle plummet more than 12 miles down to the Atlantic Ocean.

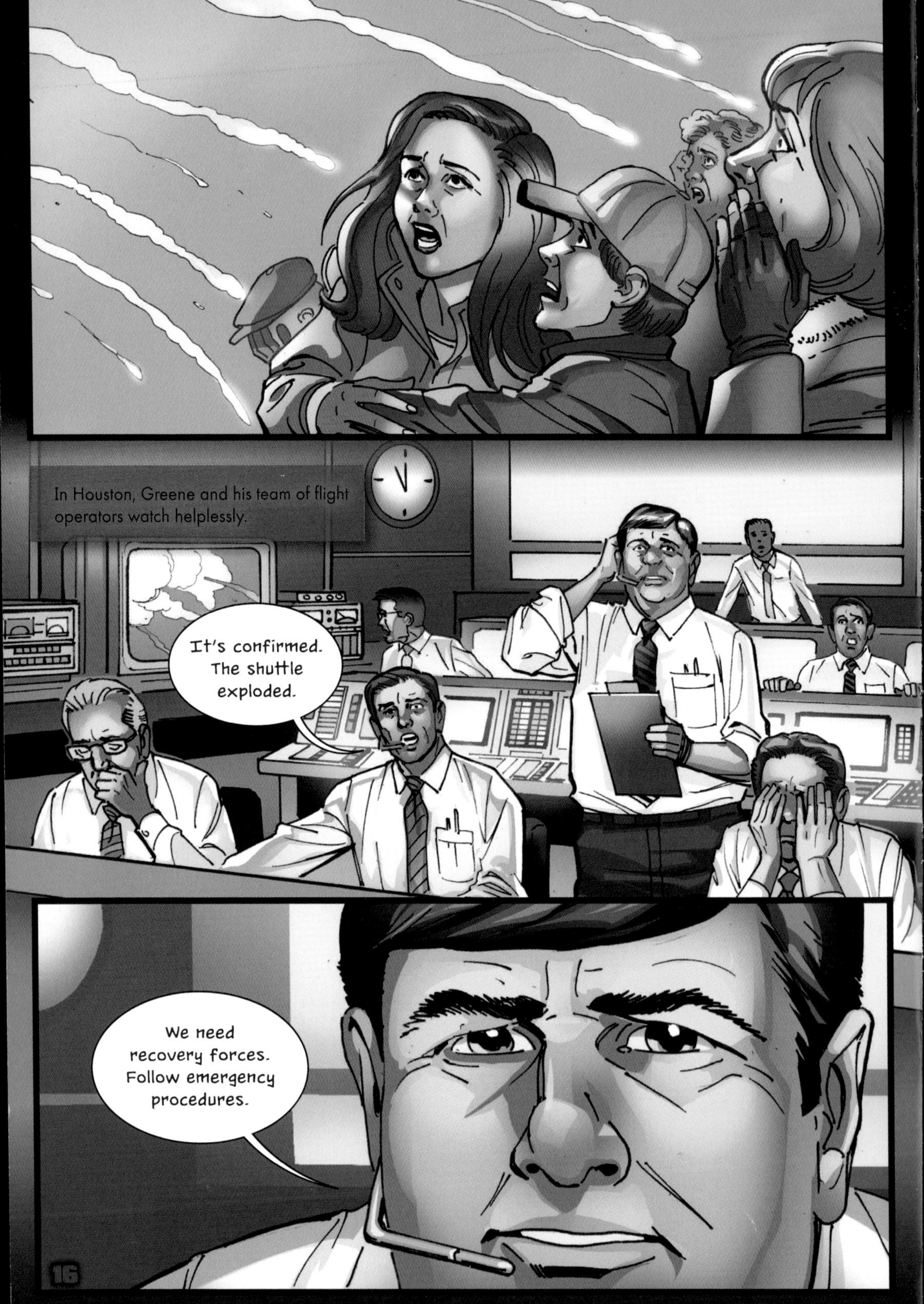
In Houston, Greene and his team of flight operators watch helplessly.
It's confirmed. The shuttle exploded.
We need recovery forces. Follow emergency procedures.

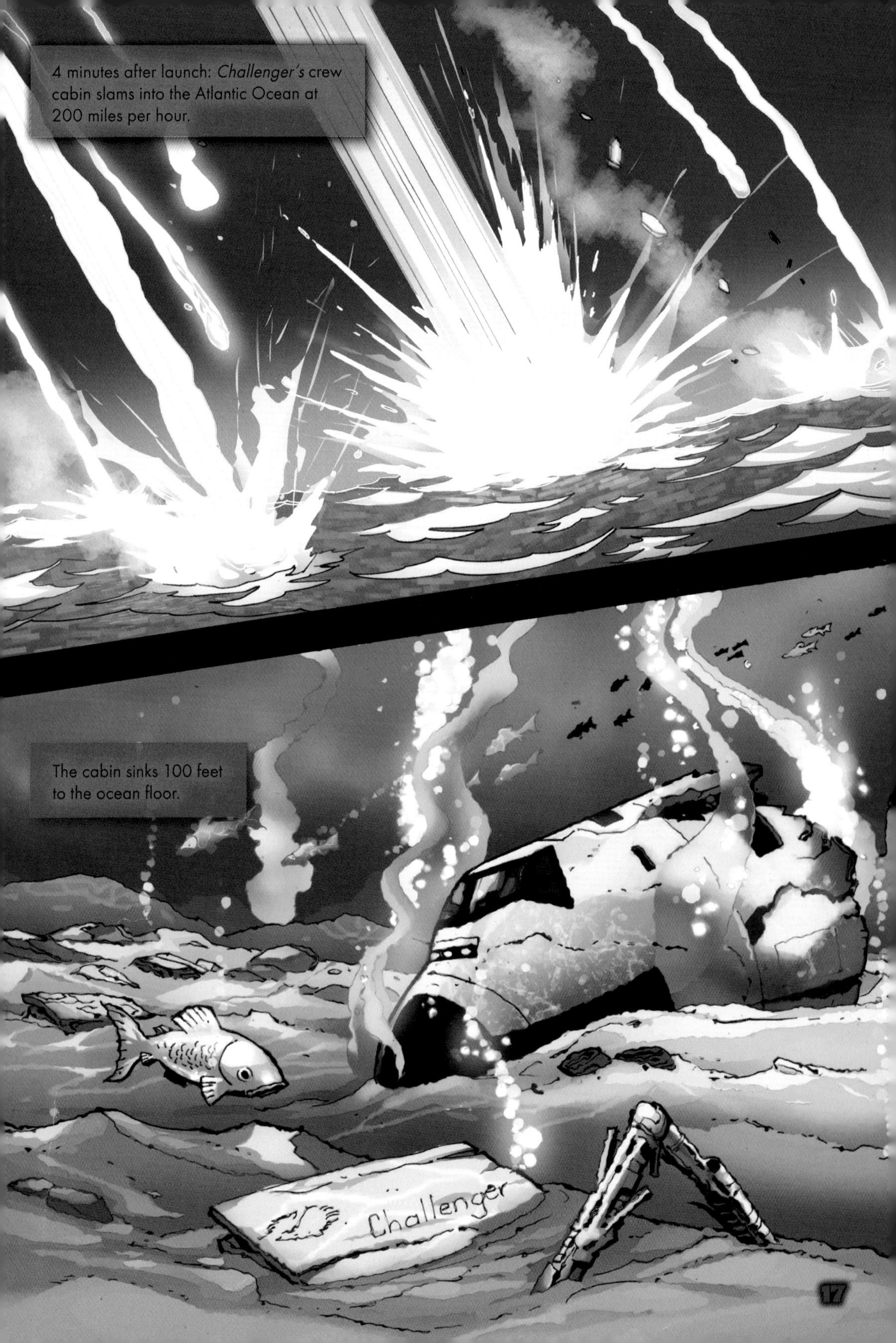
4 minutes after launch: *Challenger's* crew cabin slams into the Atlantic Ocean at 200 miles per hour.
The cabin sinks 100 feet to the ocean floor.
Challenger

Learning from Tragedy

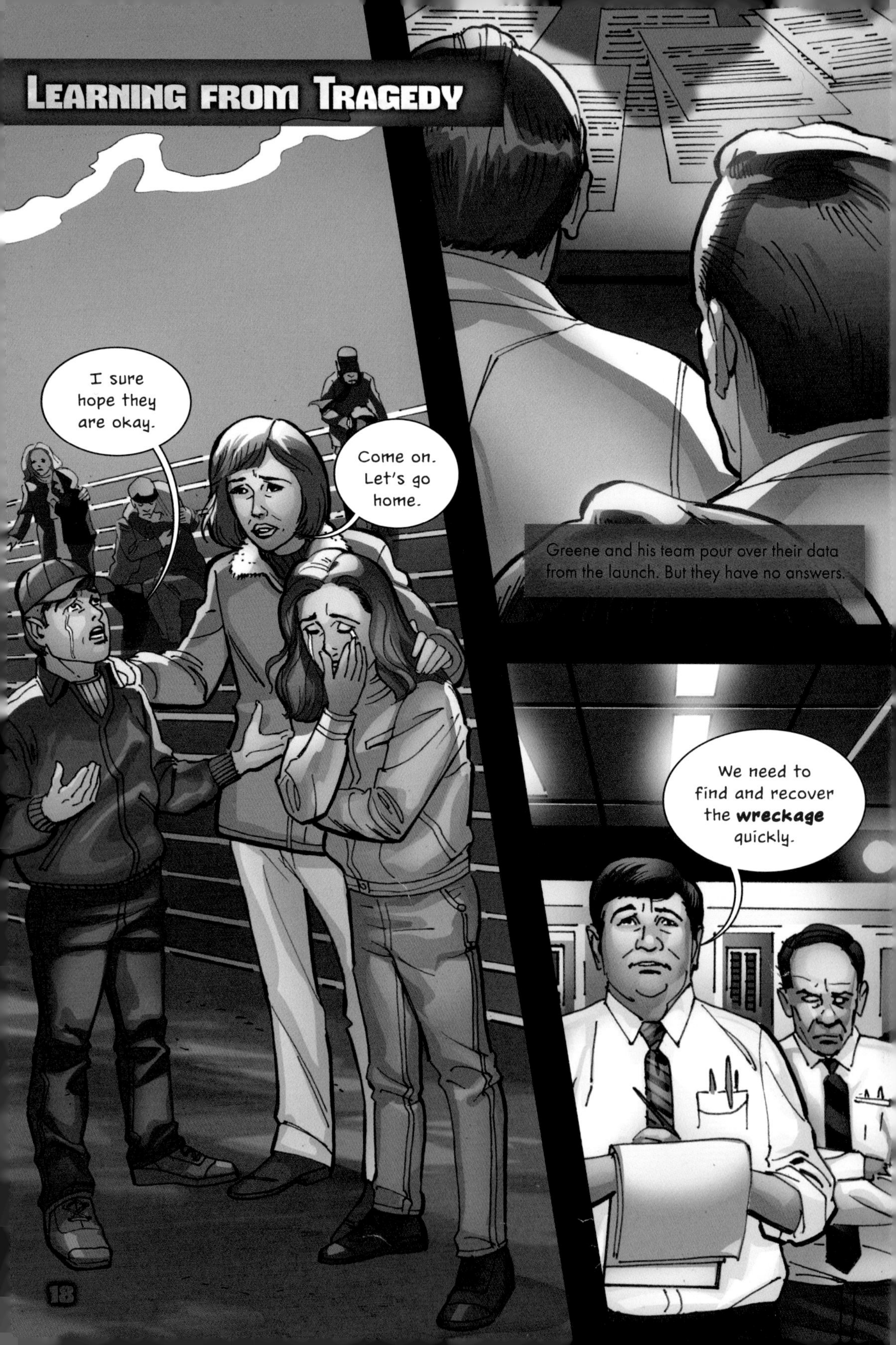

I sure hope they are okay.
Come on. Let's go home.
Greene and his team pour over their data from the launch. But they have no answers.
We need to find and recover the **wreckage** quickly.

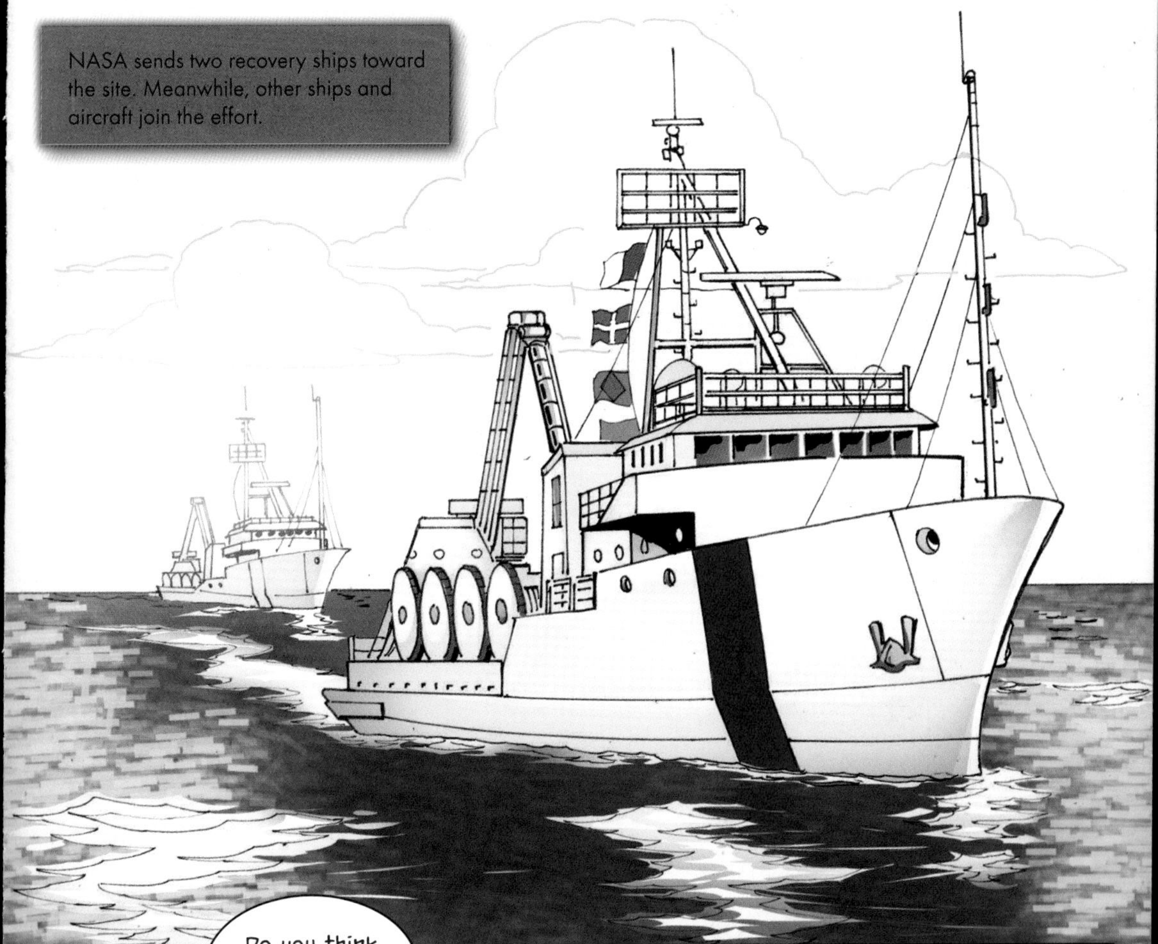
NASA sends two recovery ships toward the site. Meanwhile, other ships and aircraft join the effort.

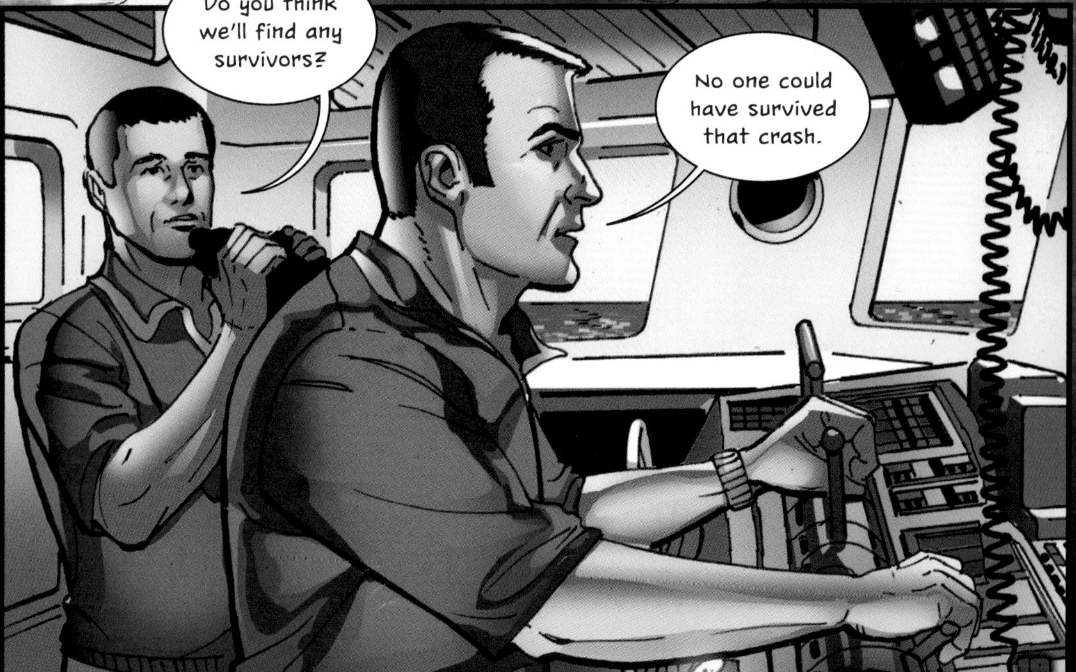
Do you think we'll find any survivors?
No one could have survived that crash.

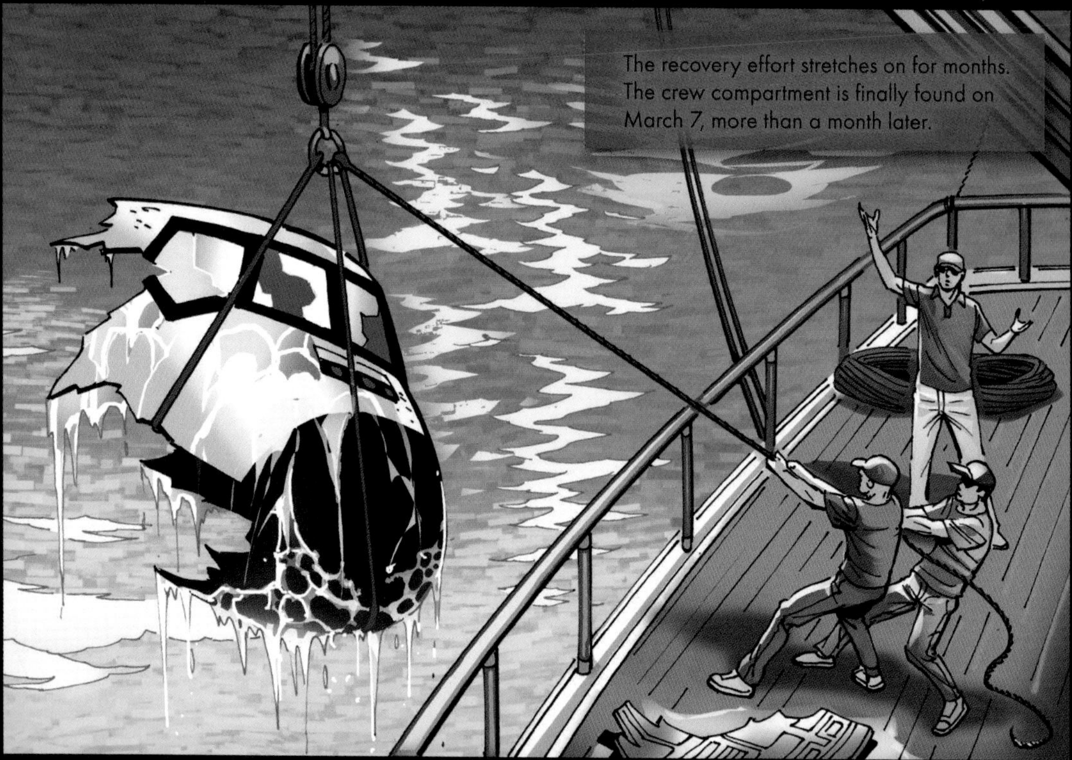
The recovery effort stretches on for months. The crew compartment is finally found on March 7, more than a month later.

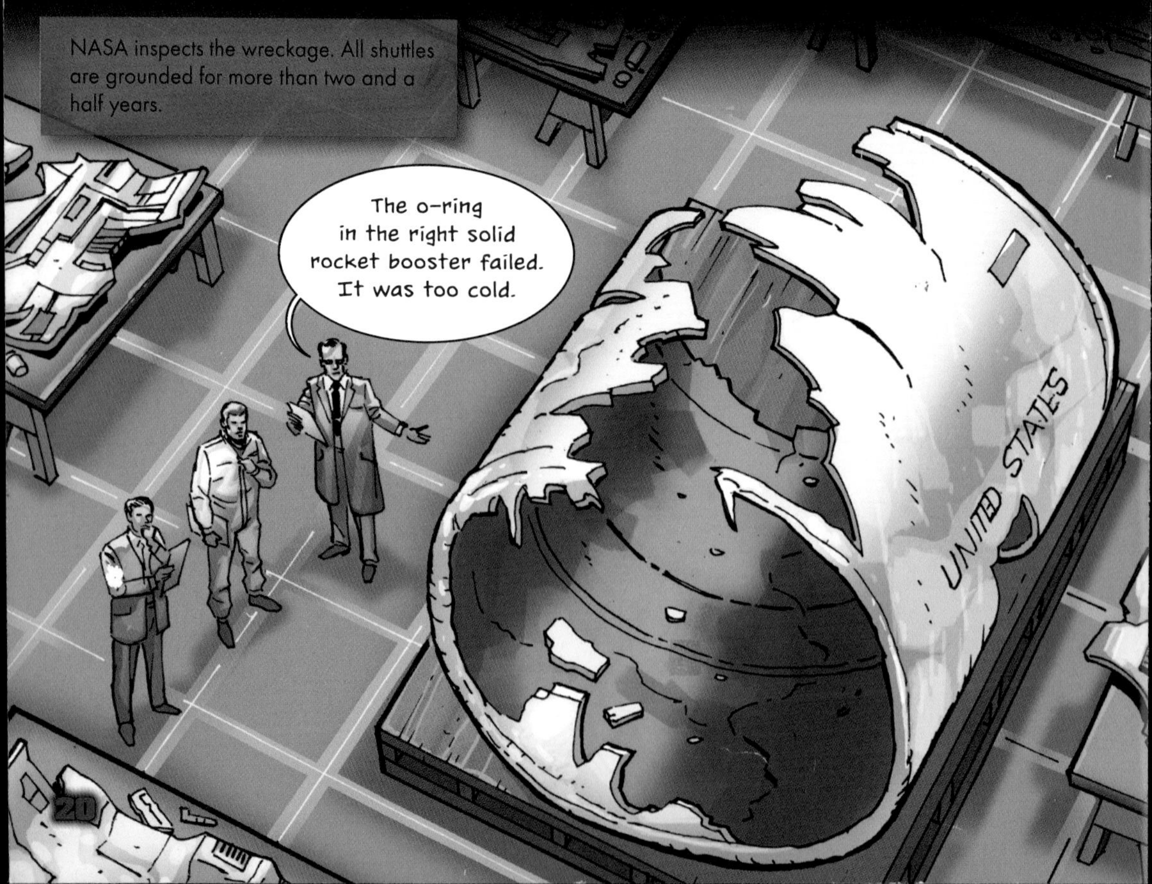
NASA inspects the wreckage. All shuttles are grounded for more than two and a half years.
The o-ring in the right solid rocket booster failed. It was too cold.
UNITED STATES

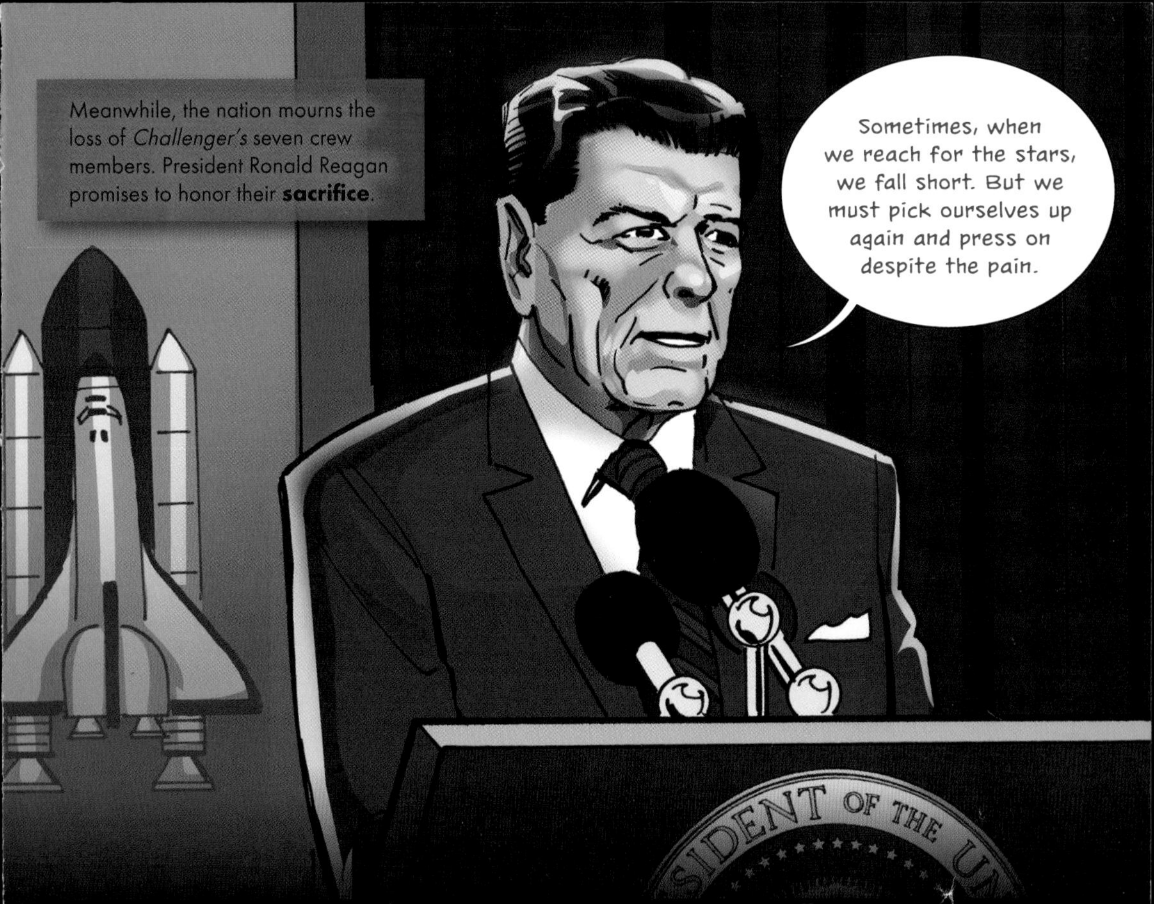
Meanwhile, the nation mourns the loss of *Challenger's* seven crew members. President Ronald Reagan promises to honor their **sacrifice**.
Sometimes, when we reach for the stars, we fall short. But we must pick ourselves up again and press on despite the pain.

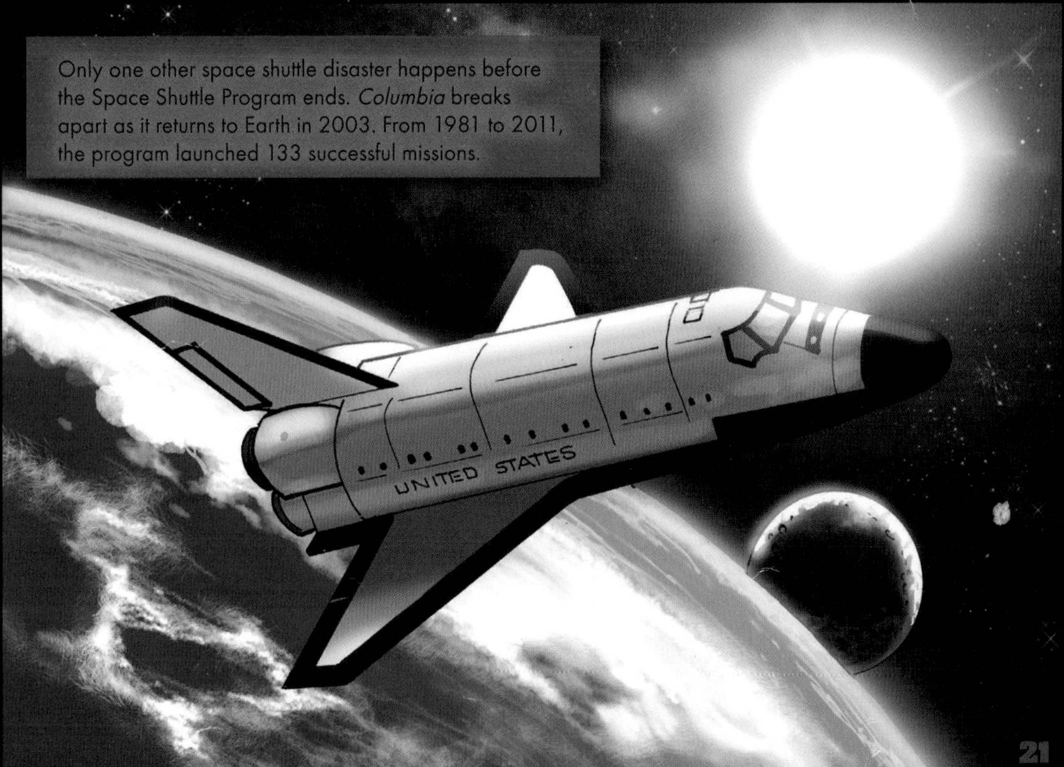
Only one other space shuttle disaster happens before the Space Shuttle Program ends. *Columbia* breaks apart as it returns to Earth in 2003. From 1981 to 2011, the program launched 133 successful missions.
UNITED STATES

MORE ABOUT THE DISASTER

- *Challenger* had nine successful missions between its first launch and the 1986 disaster.

- The *Challenger* shuttle was named after the HMS *Challenger*. In the 1870s, this British ship was the first to conduct ocean research solely for science. The space shuttle also set out to explore and learn.

- Christa McAuliffe was chosen to go to space for NASA's Teacher in Space program. She was supposed to teach lessons in space. They would have been broadcast to children across the United States.

- Barbara Morgan was chosen as Christa McAuliffe's backup in the Teacher in Space program. More than twenty years after the *Challenger* disaster, she successfully went to space and back on the shuttle *Endeavour*.

- The recovered wreckage of the *Challenger* shuttle is in Cape Canaveral, Florida. It lies in missile silos at the Air Force Station.

GLOSSARY

civilian—a person who is not part of the military or a government agency

ignite—to catch fire

mission—an important task or assignment

Mission Control—the command center for a space mission

NASA—short for the National Aeronautics and Space Administration; NASA is the agency that oversees U.S. space travel.

o-ring—a piece of a solid rocket booster that prevents gases from leaking

sacrifice—offering of oneself in service

solid rocket boosters—large rockets used to launch a space shuttle into orbit around Earth

space shuttle—a vehicle designed to travel to outer space and return to Earth safely

wreckage—the remains of something that has been badly damaged or destroyed

To Learn More

AT THE LIBRARY

Holden, Henry M. *Space Shuttle Disaster: The Tragic Mission of the Challenger*. Berkeley Heights, N.J.: Enslow Publishers, 2013.

Stone, Adam. *The Apollo 13 Mission*. Minneapolis, Minn.: Bellwether Media, 2015.

Waxman, Laura Hamilton. *Exploring Space Travel*. Minneapolis, Minn.: Lerner Publications Company, 2011.

ON THE WEB

Learning more about the *Challenger* explosion is as easy as 1, 2, 3.

1. Go to www.factsurfer.com.
2. Enter "Challenger explosion" into the search box.
3. Click the "Surf" button and you will see a list of related web sites.

With factsurfer.com, finding more information is just a click away.

INDEX